NASHVILLE PUBLIC LIBRARY

FOUNDATION

This book
made possible
through generous gifts
to the
Nashville Public Library
Foundation Book Fund

NPLF.ORG

Dentists

BY CECILIA MINDEN AND LINDA M. ARMANTROUT

Published by The Child's World®
1980 Lookout Drive • Mankato, MN 56003-1705
800-599-READ • www.childsworld.com

Acknowledgments
The Child's World®: Mary Berendes, Publishing Director
The Design Lab: Design
Jody Jensen Shaffer: Editing

Photos
2xSamara.com/Shutterstock.com: 12; Africa Studio/Shutterstock.com: 22; aimy27feb/Shutterstock.com: 13; Anna Jurkovska/Shutterstock.com: 10-11; apomares/iStock.com: 16; Bogdan Dumitru/Dreamstime.com: toothpaste; chas53/iStock.com: dentures; Creativa/Shutterstock.com: 6-7; JHershPhoto/Shutterstock.com: 17; Linda M. Armantrout: 5, 9, 15; peterfactors/Shutterstock.com: 14; PonyWang/iStock.com: cover, 1; rimglow/iStock.com: 19; S.Castelli /Shutterstock.com: 8, 20-21; Tracy Whiteside/Shutterstock.com: 4; Yarinca/iStock.com: 18

ISBN 9781626870116
LCCN 2013947288

Printed in the United States of America
Mankato, MN
December, 2013
PA02191

ABOUT THE AUTHORS

Dr. Cecilia Minden is a university professor and reading specialist with classroom and administrative experience in grades K–12. She earned her PhD in reading education from the University of Virginia.

Linda M. Armantrout received her nurse's training at Saint John's School of Nursing in Tulsa, Oklahoma. She has had many opportunities to practice nursing skills with her eight children and nine grandchildren. Linda and her husband, Glen, live in Louisiana.

CONTENTS

Hello, My Name Is Jasmine.

Hello. My name is Jasmine. Many people live and work in my neighborhood. Each of them helps the neighborhood in different ways.

I thought of all the things I like to do. I like helping others. I am good at science. I know how to take care of my body. How could I help my neighborhood when I grow up?

It is important for people to take care of their teeth.

I Could Be a Dentist!

Dentists know a lot about science. They talk to their patients and look inside their mouths. Dentists help people take care of their teeth. Best of all, dentists create happy smiles!

When Did This Job Start?
The first dental school opened in 1840 in Baltimore, Maryland. Dentists were using special instruments such as drills by 1900.

Dentists show people of all ages how to care for their teeth.

Learn About This Neighborhood Helper!

The best way to learn is to ask questions. Words such as *who*, *what*, *where*, *when*, and *why* will help me learn about being a dentist.

Where Can I Learn More?
American Dental Association
Commission on Dental Accreditation
211 E. Chicago Avenue
Chicago, IL 60611

American Dental Education Association
1400 K Street NW, Suite 1100
Washington, DC 20005

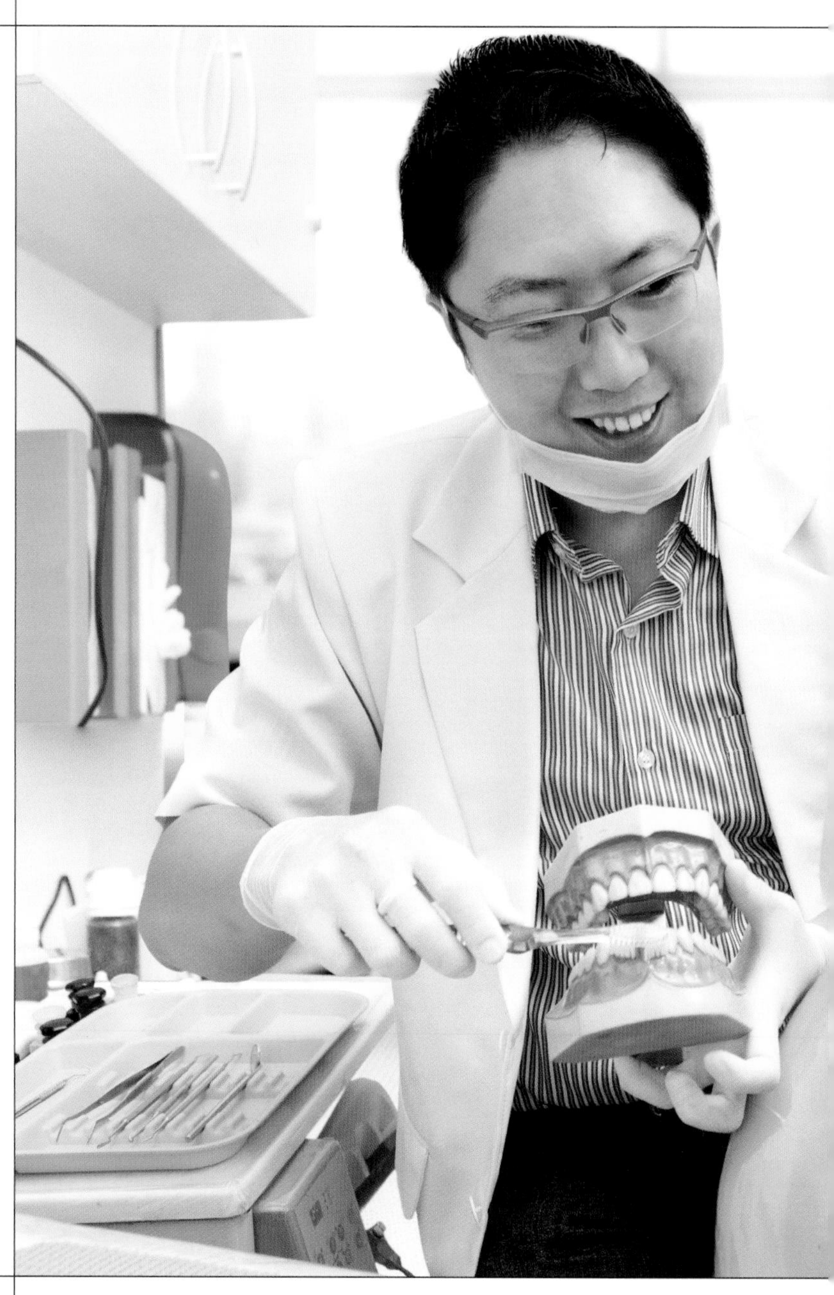

Asking a dentist questions will help you learn more about the job.

Who Can Become a Dentist?

Boys and girls who are good at science may want to become dentists. People who want to be dentists also need to know how to ask questions and listen carefully to the answers. Dentists and patients work together to keep teeth strong and clean.

Dentists are important neighborhood helpers. They show people how to take care of their mouths. Dentists help people stay healthy.

How Can I Explore This Job?

Ask your dentist questions about her job the next time you go for a checkup. How did she decide to become a dentist? How long has she been a dentist? What does she like best about her job?

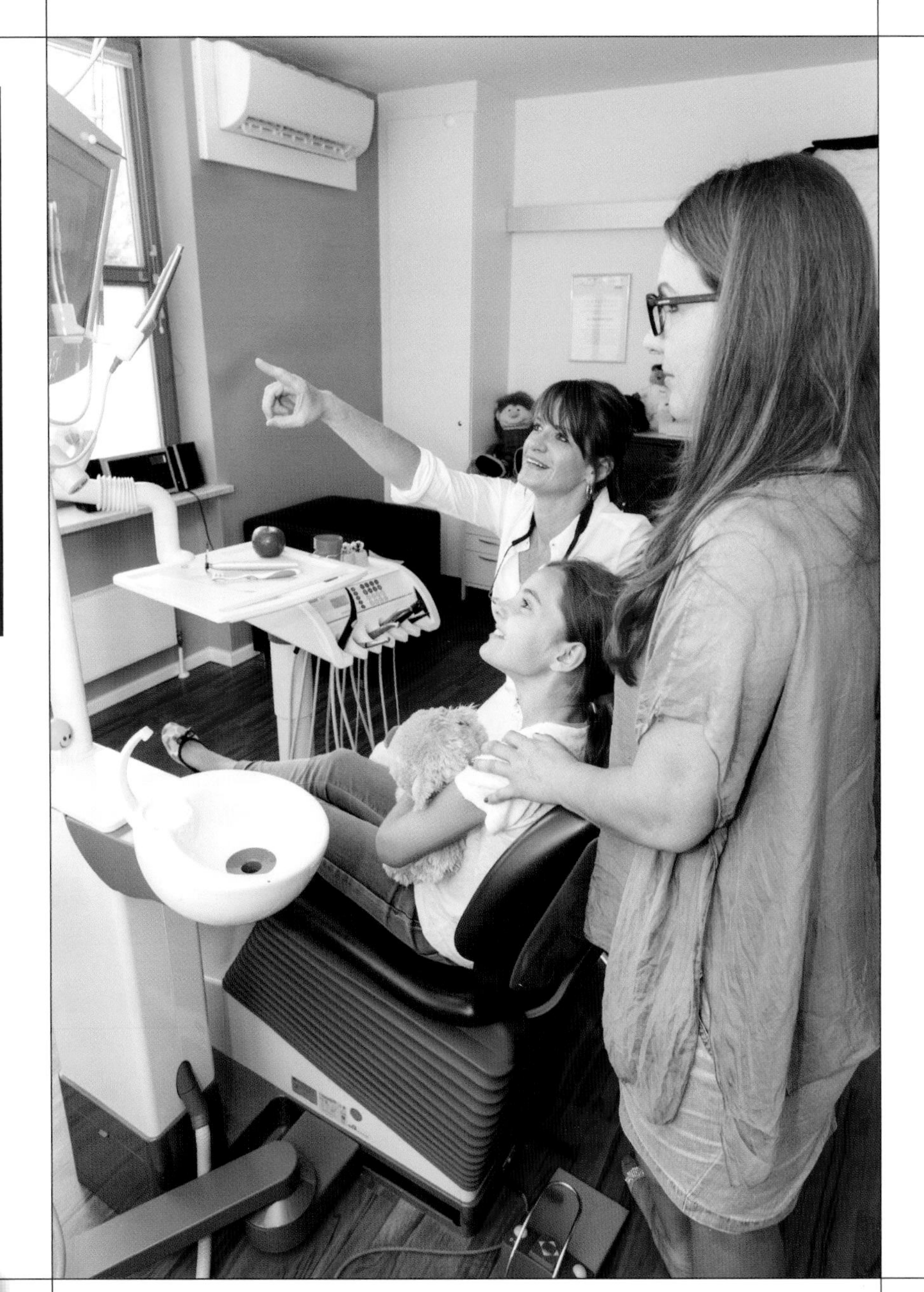

Dentists work with families to keep everyone's teeth healthy.

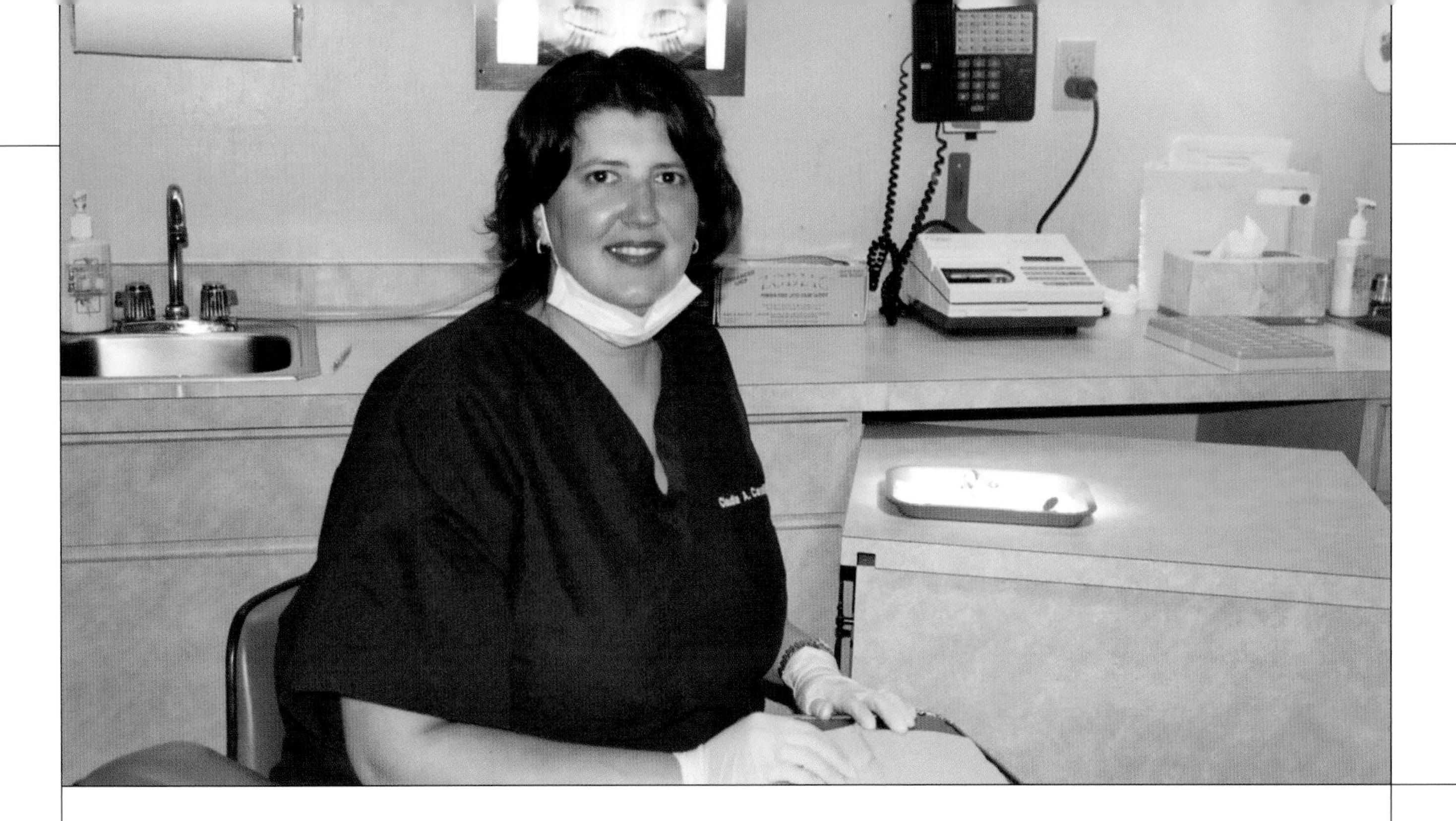

Meet a Dentist!

This is Dr. Claudia Cavallino. Dr. Claudia is a **pediatric** dentist in Metarie, Louisiana. All of her patients are children. When she is not in the office, she likes to read, travel, and go to movies with her friends.

How Many Dentists Are There?
About 153,000 people work as dentists in the United States.

Dr. Claudia helps children take care of their teeth.

Where Can I Learn to Be a Dentist?

Dr. Claudia first went to college. Then she went to the Louisiana State University School of Dentistry for four years. She learned all about taking care of teeth.

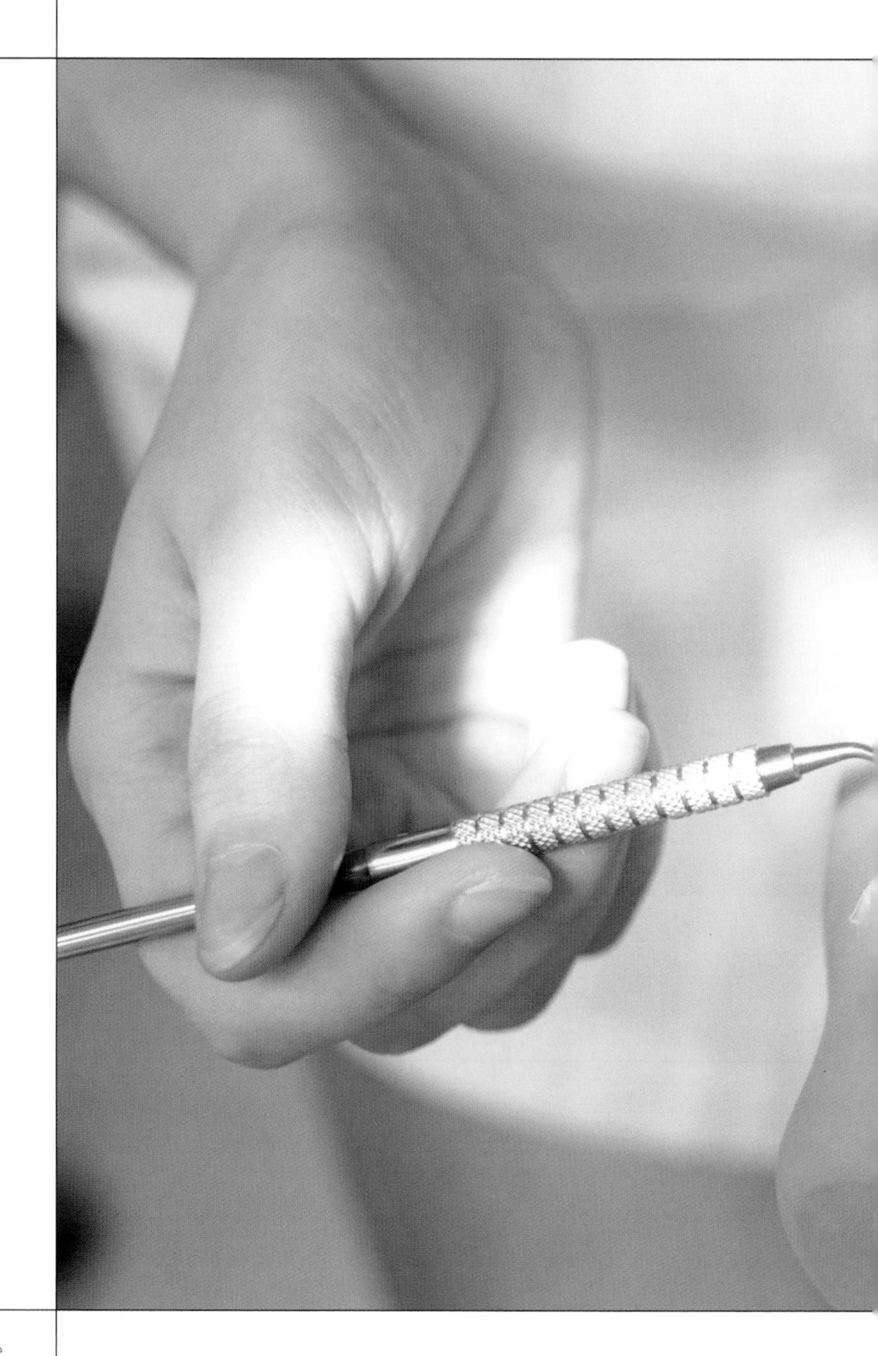

Students in dental school use models. They practice how they will one day work on people's teeth.

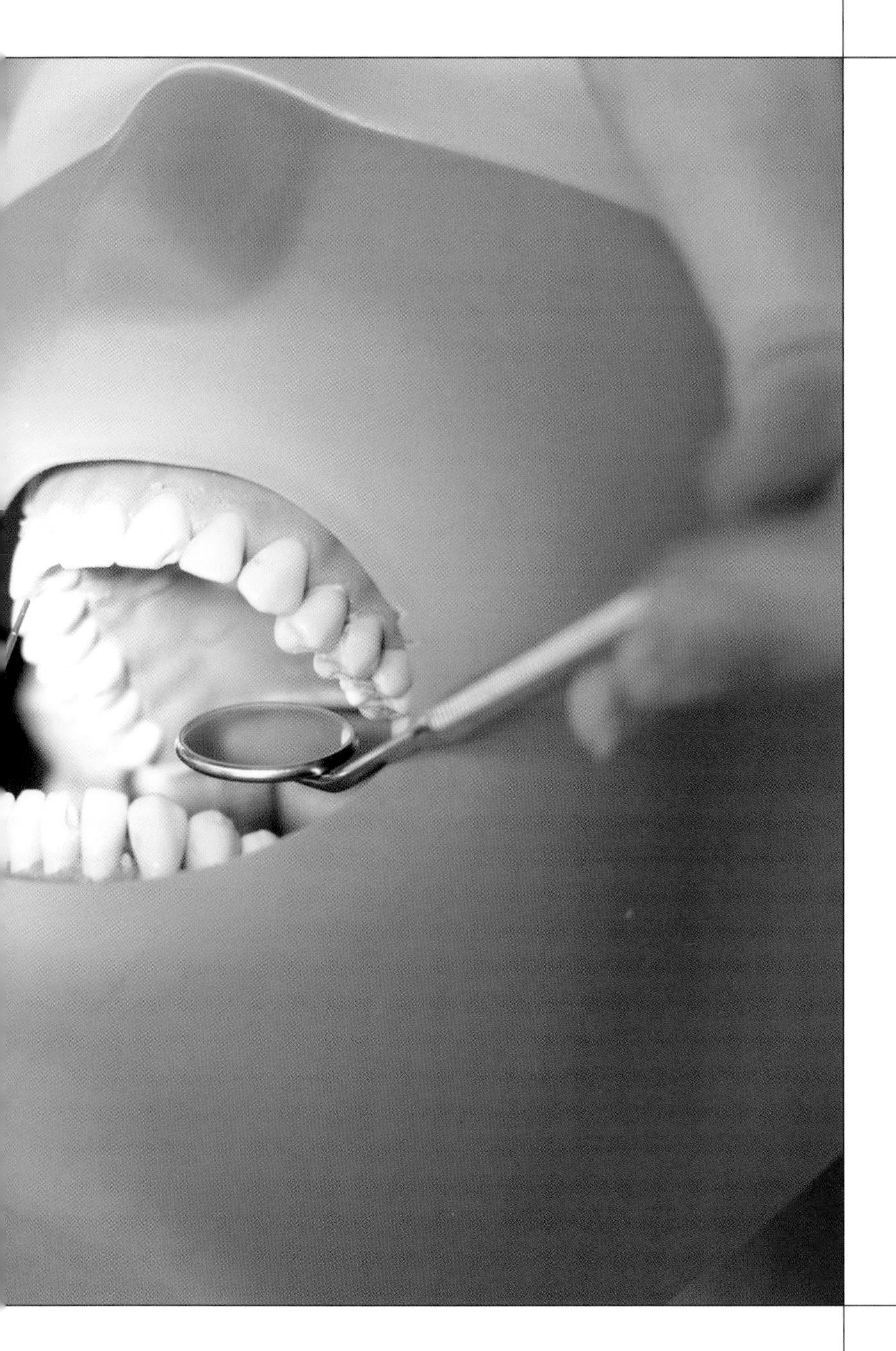

Dentists need to be good readers and writers. They also take many courses in science and math.

How big is the inside of your mouth? How big are your teeth? Dentists must work with their hands in very small spaces to keep teeth healthy.

How Much School Will I Need?

Dentists must first get a degree from a four-year college. They then go to dental school for four more years. Dentists must pass tests given by the state where they work. They are then given a license by the state.

Dentists use different mirrors and explorers to do their job.

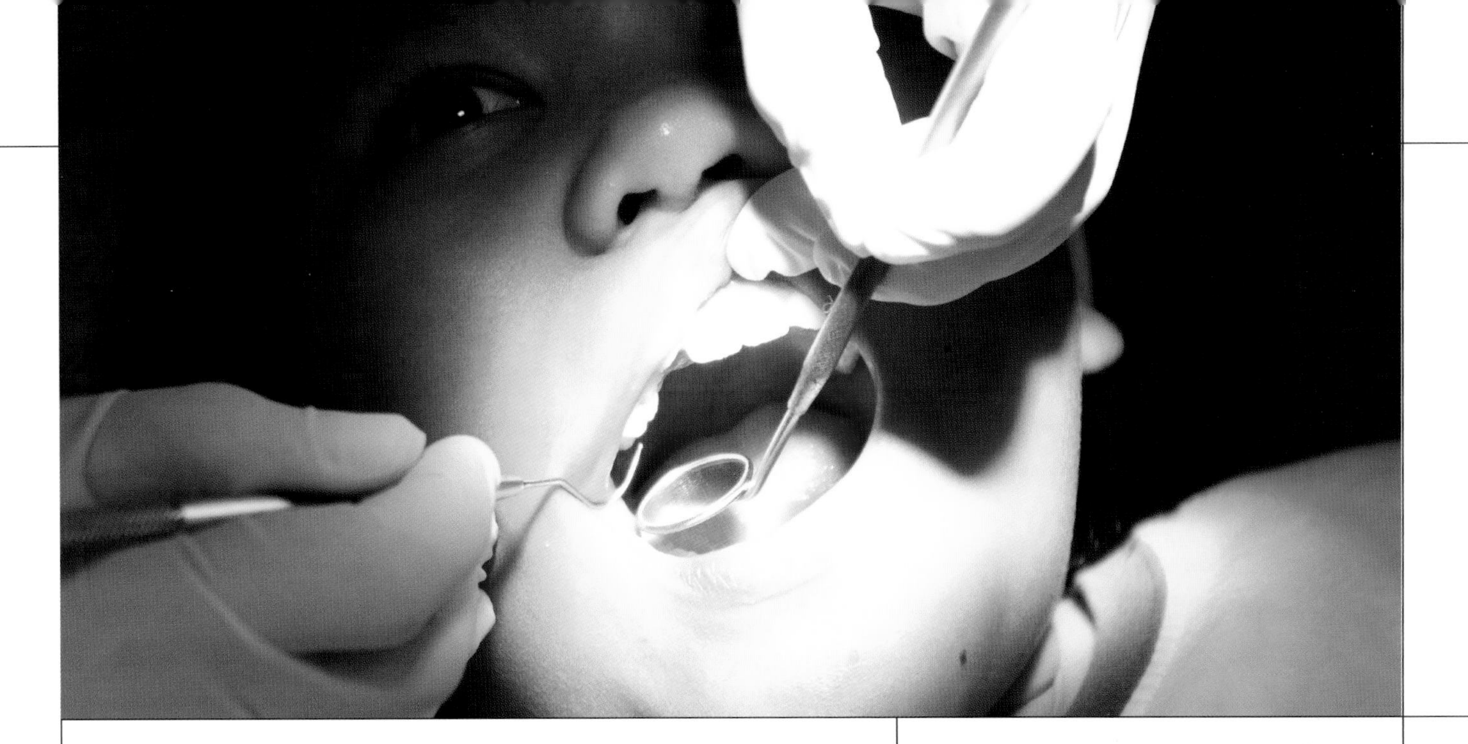

What Does a Dentist Need to Do the Job?

Dr. Claudia checks people's teeth with a mirror and an explorer. The mirror is bent at an angle so she can see behind each tooth. Dr. Claudia touches each tooth with the explorer to check for **cavities** or cracks.

What Are Some Instruments I Will Use?

- Drill
- Explorer
- Mouth mirror
- Polisher

Dentists use an explorer and a mirror to carefully check each tooth.

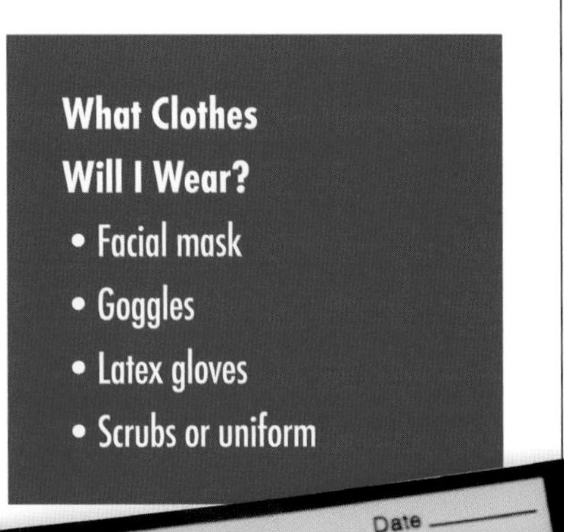

What Clothes Will I Wear?

- Facial mask
- Goggles
- Latex gloves
- Scrubs or uniform

Dentists also check for broken teeth and sores in the mouth. Dr. Claudia needs to know how to use many instruments to find and fix different problems. She sometimes uses an **X-ray machine** to take pictures of people's teeth. These pictures help her find problems she might not see on her own.

Dentists sometimes take X-rays of people's teeth.

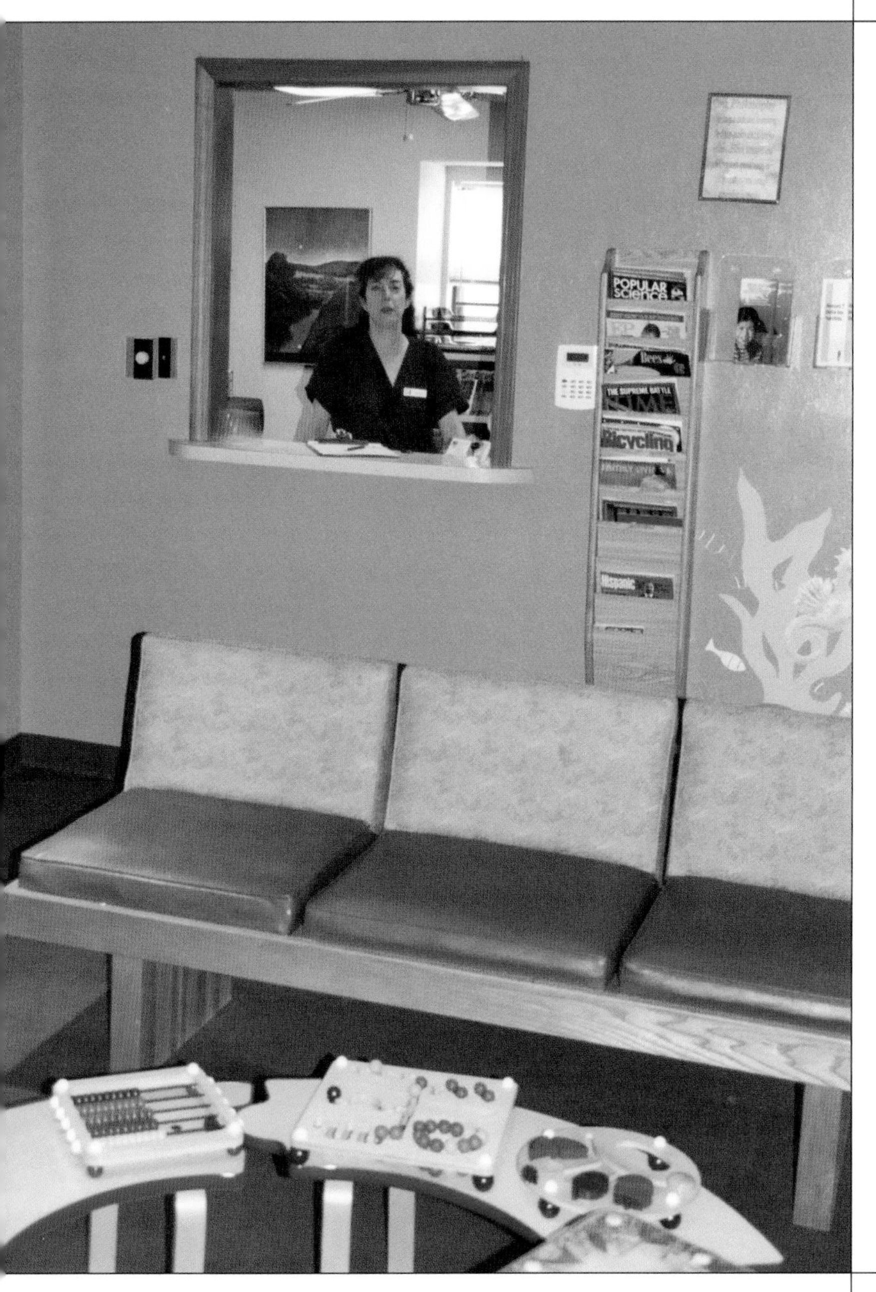

People usually wait in an outer room until their dentist is ready to see them.

Where Does a Dentist Work?

Most dentists work in an office with a number of different rooms. People who visit Dr. Claudia's office wait in an outer room until she is ready to see them.

What's It Like Where I'll Work?

Dentist offices are clean, quiet, and well-lighted. They are often brightly decorated. Many have TVs for patients to watch.

Dr. Claudia sees her patients in a room called the operatory. People sit in a chair while she checks their teeth. There is a light over the chair. It helps Dr. Claudia see inside her patients' mouths.

How Much Money Will I Make?
Most dentists make more than $125,000 a year.

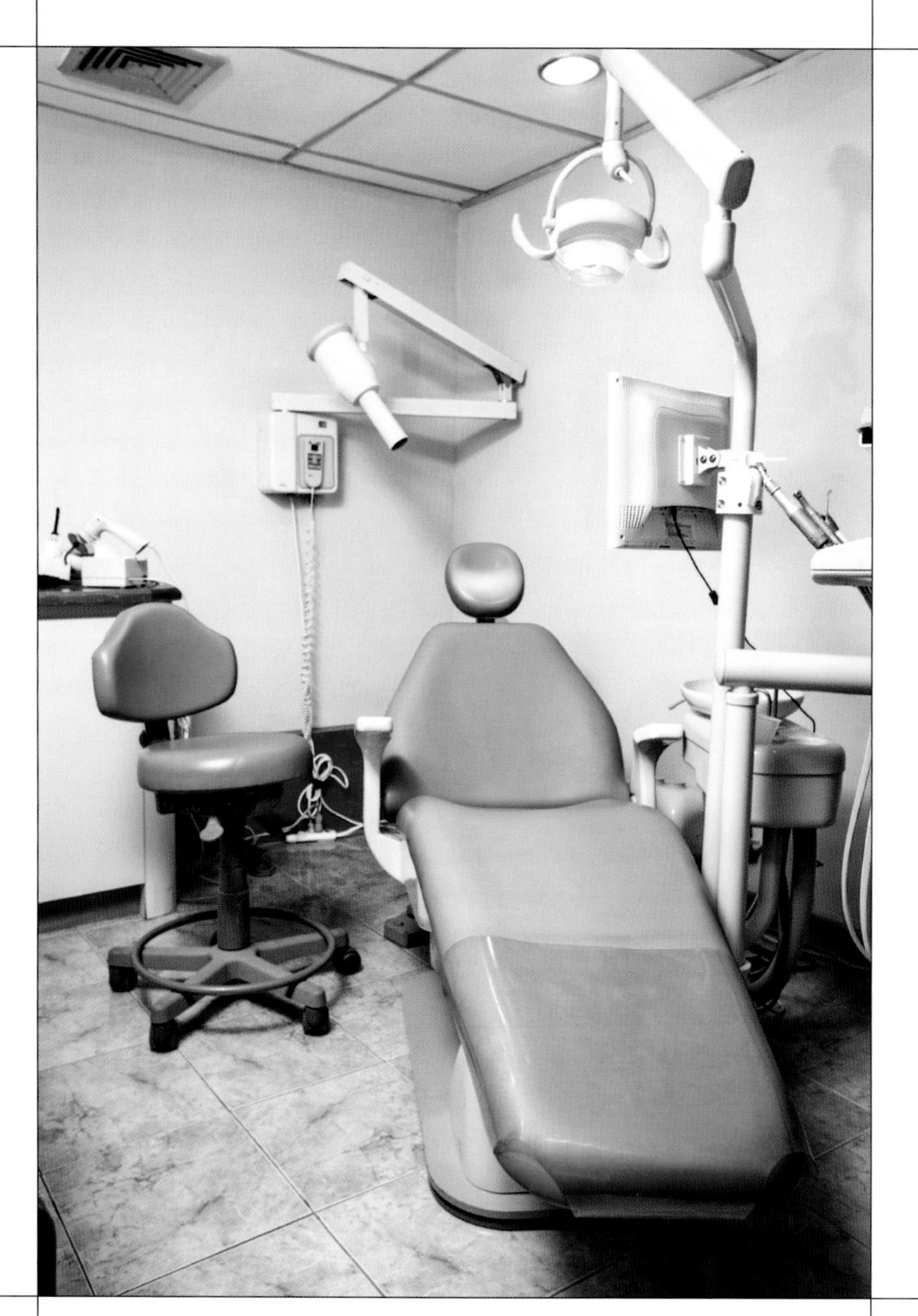

Patients relax in a big chair while the dentist works.

Who Works with Dentists?

Dr. Claudia has important helpers. A dental hygienist works with her in the operatory. The dental hygienist helps Dr. Claudia clean people's teeth and take X-rays.

Dr. Claudia also works with another dentist. Dr. Marvin Cavallino is her father!

What other Jobs Might I Like?

- Dental assistant
- Dental hygienist
- Orthodontist
- Physician

Dental hygienists often clean people's teeth.

Flossing your teeth is a good way to get rid of plaque.

When Did People Start Using Dental Floss?

Did you know that another dentist from Louisiana helped develop dental floss? Dr. Levi Spear Parmly made dental floss from silk threads in 1815. Dental floss helps get the **plaque** out from between your teeth. This keeps cavities away and is good for your gums.

How Might My Job Change?
Many new dentists work in offices for other dentists. They sometimes later start their own offices. Some dentists become teachers in dental schools.

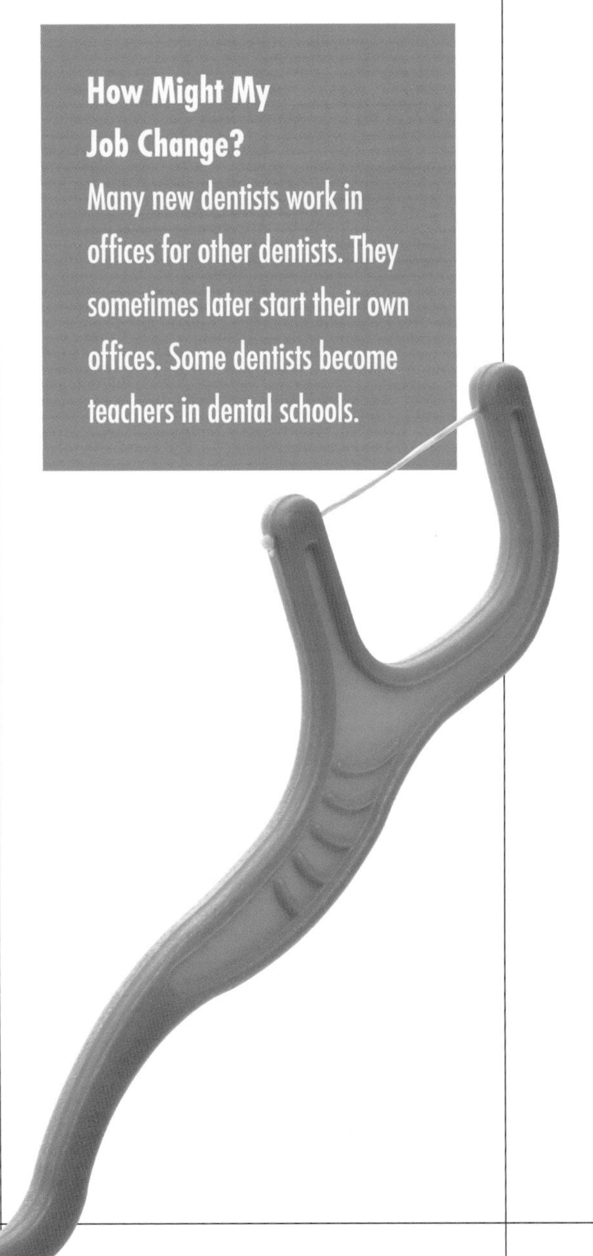

Many people use flossing picks to floss their teeth.

I Want to Be a Dentist!

I think being a dentist would be a great way to be a neighborhood helper. Someday I may be the person helping you take care of your teeth!

Is This Job Growing?
The need for dentists will grow more slowly than other jobs.

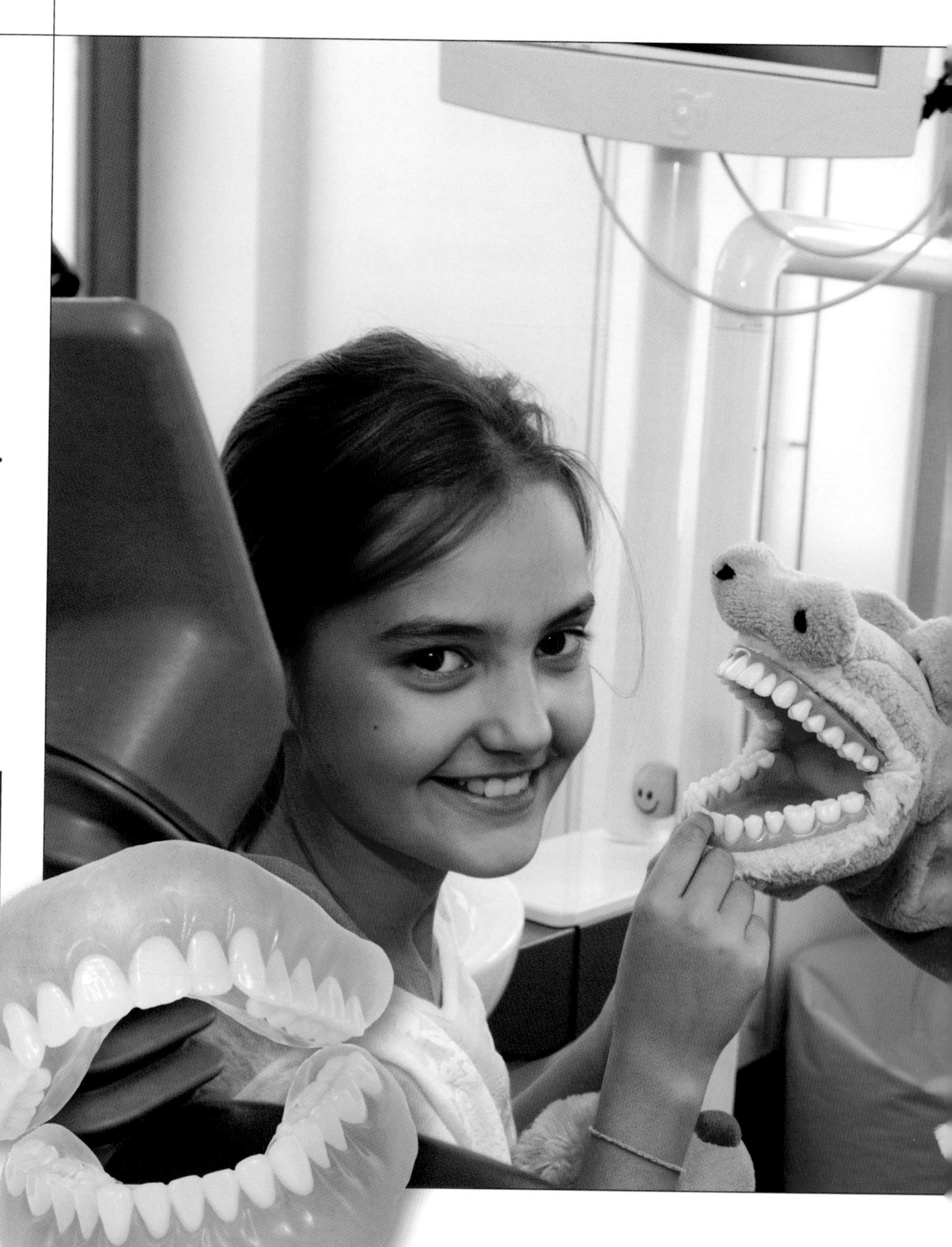

Open wide! Perhaps one day you'll be a dentist.

Why Don't You Try Being a Dentist?

Do you think you would like to be a dentist? A dentist teaches others how to take care of their teeth. Look at the picture on page 22. Can you name each of the instruments a dentist needs to keep your teeth healthy? Can you tell a friend how to use each of these instruments?

I Didn't Know That!
Lucy Hobbs became the first woman to graduate from dental school in the United States. She graduated in 1866.

Dentists often use (from left to right)

- *dental floss*
- *a mouth mirror*
- *toothbrush*
- *explorer*
- *a chisel*
- *scraper*

GLOSSARY

cavities (KAV-it-eez) holes that occur in teeth when they start to decay

pediatric (pee-dee-AH-trik) a type of doctor or dentist who only works with children

plaque (PLAK) a soft, sticky substance that forms on teeth and contains bacteria

X-ray machine (EKS-ray muh-SHEEN) a machine used to take pictures of people's bones and teeth

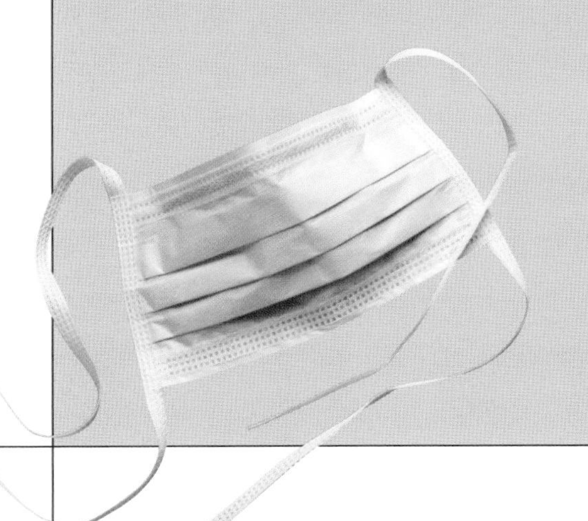

LEARN MORE ABOUT DENTISTS

BOOKS

Fremont, Eleanor. *A Visit to the Dentist.* New York: Simon Spotlight/ Nick Jr., 2002.

Hughes, Monica. *First Visit to the Dentist.* Chicago: Raintree, 2004.

Keller, Laurie. *Open Wide: Tooth School Inside.* New York: Henry Holt, 2000.

Nelson, Kristin L. *Dentists.* Minneapolis: Lerner Publications, 2005.

WEB SITES

Visit our home page for lots of links about dentists:

www.childsworld.com/links

Note to Parents, Teachers, and Librarians: We routinely check our Web links to make sure they're safe, active sites—so encourage your readers to check them out!

INDEX